CGP has Year 6 Grammar practice sorted!

The best way for pupils to improve their Grammar in Year 6 (ages 10-11) is by doing as much practice as they can.

That's where this book comes in. It's packed with questions that'll test them on all the crucial Grammar skills, including those introduced for the first time in Year 6.

And there's more! Everything is perfectly matched to the National Curriculum and we've included answers at the back. Enjoy!

What CGP is all about

Our sole aim here at CGP is to produce the highest quality books — carefully written, immaculately presented and dangerously close to being funny.

Then we work our socks off to get them out to you — at the cheapest possible prices.

Published by CGP

Editors
Heather Cowley, Catherine Heygate, Gabrielle Richardson, Hayley Shaw, Sam Summers
With thanks to Keith Blackhall for the proofreading.

ISBN: 978 1 78294 122 4

Clipart from Corel®
Printed by Elanders Ltd, Newcastle upon Tyne.
Based on the classic CGP style created by Richard Parsons.

Text, design, layout and original illustrations © Coordination Group Publications Ltd. (CGP) 2022
All rights reserved.

Photocopying this book is not permitted, even if you have a CLA licence.
Extra copies are available from CGP with next day delivery • 0800 1712 712 • www.cgpbooks.co.uk

Contents

Section 1 – Word Types

Nouns 4
Adjectives 5
Verbs 6
Adverbs 7
Synonyms and Antonyms 8
Determiners 10
Pronouns 11

Section 2 – Phrases and Clauses

Phrases 12
Clauses 14

Section 3 – Linking Ideas

Conjunctions 15
Linking Paragraphs with Adverbials 16
Linking Paragraphs Using Repetition 17
Using Ellipsis 18

Section 4 – Tenses

Present Tense and Past Tense 19
Present and Past Progressive 20
The Perfect Form 21

Section 5 – Sentence Structure

Subject and Object 22
Passive and Active Voice 24

Section 6 – Writing Style

Formal and Informal Writing 27
Writing for Your Audience 30
Standard and Non-Standard English 32

Glossary 36
Answers 37

Section 1 — Word Types

Nouns

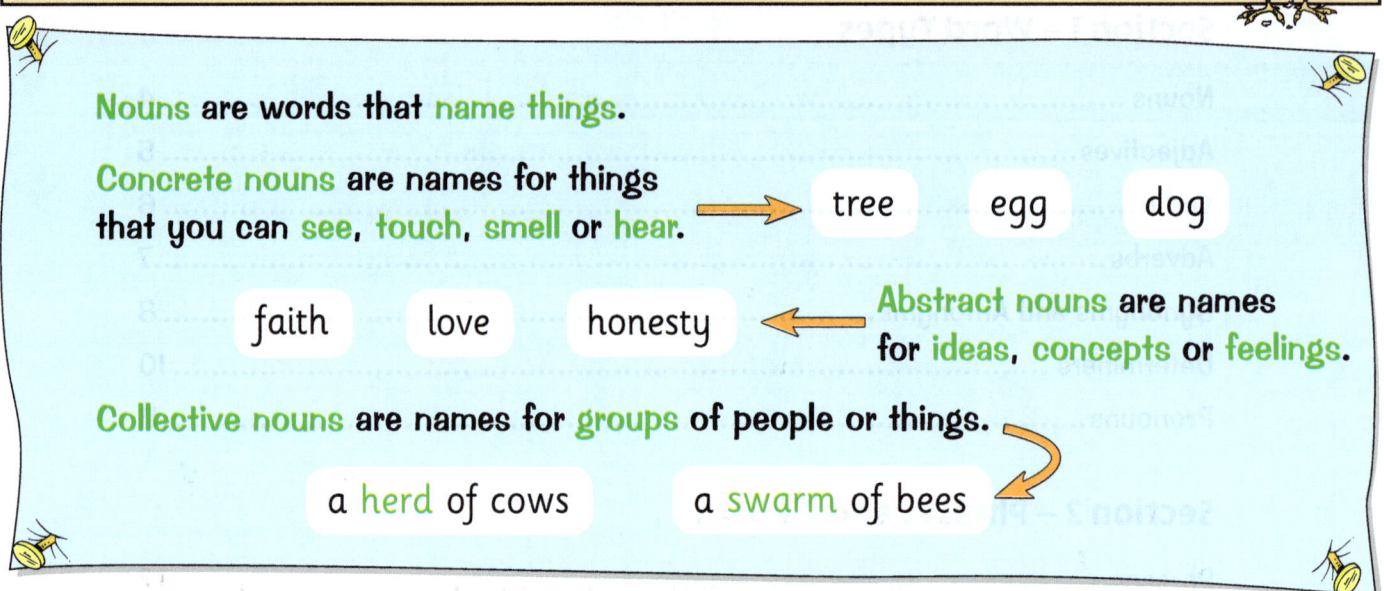

Nouns are words that name things.

Concrete nouns are names for things that you can see, touch, smell or hear. → tree egg dog

faith love honesty ← Abstract nouns are names for ideas, concepts or feelings.

Collective nouns are names for groups of people or things.
a herd of cows   a swarm of bees

---

1) Underline the concrete nouns and circle the abstract nouns in the passage below.

There's been so much excitement about going to the zoo. We're all eager to see the lions, but we're especially looking forward to seeing the monkeys. Ella has been scared of animals since childhood though, so she'll need to find some courage to come along.

2) Rewrite the sentences below replacing the underlined nouns with your own nouns.

Everyone feels so much <u>boredom</u> about doing more drawings of <u>flowers</u>.

....

The <u>colony</u> of <u>ants</u> moves really slowly along the <u>path</u>.

....

A group of <u>wolves</u> could be called a <u>pack</u>.

....

 Can you spot a proper noun on this page?

Adjectives

Adjectives are words that tell us more about a noun.

the complex question

a fearless, courageous hero

More than one adjective can describe a noun.

1 Underline the adjectives in the passage below.

It was a cold, dark evening in Murky Lane. A howling wind rushed between the leafless trees and torrential rain pounded against the walls of the little cottages. Jittery roof tiles began to rattle and creaking gates swung violently back and forth, crashing against tired, old gateposts.

2 Add your own adjectives to the sentence below.

The .... sun shone brightly over the .... valley and the .... cows stood munching the .... grass.

3 Write one sentence using all of the adjectives below.

silly   bossy   nasty

....

....

Now Try This Write a description of your school. Underline all the adjectives you've used.

Section 1 — Word Types

Verbs

Verbs are **doing** or **being** words. → The woman digs with a spade.
→ I enjoy swimming.

Modal verbs can show how **possible** or **certain** something is.
→ The train should be here in 5 minutes.

1 Circle the correct form of each verb to finish these sentences.

Laurie often go / goes to the shop and buy / buys some bread.

We always visits / visit Habeeb at the weekend and takes / take him out.

The cows eats / eat the grass and watch / watches the walkers go by.

2 Write three sentences using the verbs and subjects below.

1 ....

2 ....

3 ....

3 Underline the modal verb in each sentence. Then tick the sentence which shows that you are most likely to have pizza.

I might have pizza for dinner tomorrow. ☐

I shall have pizza for dinner tomorrow. ☐

 Write down as many verbs as you can in one minute.

Section 1 — Word Types

Adverbs

Adverbs are words that describe **verbs**, **adjectives** and **other adverbs**.

I carefully opened the door.

He played very badly.

'carefully' is the adverb.

The game was terribly boring.

Some adverbs show how **possible** or **certain** something is.

I will surely go.   I will possibly go.

1 Add your own adverbs to the sentences below.

Jarome .... decided to book a holiday to Wales.

The girls .... passed a note to the boys.

Mum and Dad are .... pleased with me.

The test was .... difficult.

I will .... tell Katie the truth tomorrow.

The teacher jumped .... onto the bus.

2 Write one sentence using the two adverbs below.

really   probably

....

....

 Can you write a sentence using two of your own adverbs?

Section 1 — Word Types

Synonyms and Antonyms

Synonyms are words that mean the same thing. → glad and happy   small and little

loud and quiet   short and tall ← Antonyms are words that mean the opposite to each other.

To help find synonyms or antonyms, remember that they are always the same word type.

new and modern ← synonyms — two adjectives

antonyms — two adverbs → loudly and quietly

1) Draw lines to match the words below that mean the opposite.

front   big   hot   small
cold   dry   wet   back

2) Circle the correct synonyms in the sentences below.

Marvin feels drowsy — he's just so <u>alert</u> / <u>sleepy</u> today.

They live in a huge house — it's simply <u>enormous</u> / <u>tiny</u>.

The party was quite rowdy — people kept saying how <u>noisy</u> / <u>quiet</u> it was.

3) Add the correct word from the box to the sentences below.

> abundant / sparse   arrogant / humble   curious / normal

She always exaggerates her achievements — she's so ....

I think Humphrey is a bit strange — his behaviour is very ....

There are few birds around here. In fact, their numbers are ....

Section 1 — Word Types

4 Complete the crossword with antonyms for each word.

Across
1. last
2. sad
3. late
4. low
5. correct

Down 1. slow   2. easy   3. give   4. huge   5. poor

Remember — you're looking for words that mean the opposite.

5 Put the words on the right next to the correct word type. Then write a synonym and an antonym for each.

simple   quickly

Adjective: ....   Adverb: ....

Synonym: ....   Synonym: ....

Antonym: ....   Antonym: ....

6 Write a sentence using a synonym for the word below.

close

....

Write a sentence using an antonym for the word below.

nasty

....

Now Try This How many synonyms can you think of for the word 'long'?

Section 1 — Word Types

Determiners

Determiners go in front of nouns.

They can tell you whether a noun is specific or general.

 this jumper   those flowers   an egg   a present

They have lots of purposes. For example, they can tell you who owns something or how many of something there are.

→ her grapes
→ three aliens

You can use the determiners 'which', 'what' and 'whose' in questions. → Whose spaceship is it?

1 Complete these sentences by adding the missing <u>determiners</u>.

Use a different determiner each time.

.... key opens .... door?

The seagull stole .... chips from .... person over there.

I read .... book and would like to ask .... questions.

2 <u>Underline</u> the <u>determiners</u> in the sentences below.

That dog wants to eat this sandwich I brought for my lunch.

Which shoes should I wear for your birthday party this afternoon?

Today, some chickens escaped from their coop and ran into the village.

3 Add a different <u>determiner</u> and <u>noun</u> to each sentence below.

To make the biscuits, you will need ....

I must remember to take .... with me tomorrow.

Jonah couldn't believe he'd finally seen ....

 Use as many determiners as you can in one sentence.

Section 1 — Word Types

Pronouns

Pronouns are words that you use to replace nouns.

Sonal and Abed annoyed us and then they invited themselves for tea.

Relative pronouns are words like 'who' and 'which'. They are used to join two parts of a sentence together.

'us', 'they' and 'themselves' are all pronouns.

It was Nyasha and Gabija who won the competition.

1 Use the pronouns to finish the story. Use each pronoun once.

| us | which | whose | who | we |

My dog Rover hates going for walks along the path .... runs by the canal. When .... walk there, he barks a lot, especially when he sees Mr Mildew, ... Poodle then starts woofing back at us. After a while, Mrs Waterweed, ... lives in a canal boat, always opens her window and shouts at ....

2 Underline the pronouns in the sentences below.

Carrie decided to do it herself.

Some stories are fictional, others are based on real events.

The dog scratched itself when nobody was looking.

The children tasted all of the cakes but thought theirs were the best.

 Write five sentences about your family.
Use a different relative pronoun in each one.

Section 1 — Word Types

Section 2 — Phrases and Clauses

Phrases

A **phrase** is a part of a sentence that either doesn't have a verb, **or** doesn't have a subject (some phrases might have **neither**).

on the wall   hundreds of spotty dogs

A **preposition phrase** is a phrase that starts with a **preposition**.

by the pond   around the park

Prepositions can tell you **where** things are in relation to each other. They can also tell you **when** or **why** things happen.

1) Put a <u>tick</u> next to the groups of words below which are <u>phrases</u>.

He met Adnan ☐   under the bed ☐   after I'd eaten ☐

in the garden ☐   big birds of prey ☐   through the woods ☐

if it rains ☐   Kim goes fishing ☐   on the top shelf ☐

2) <u>Circle</u> the <u>preposition</u> and <u>underline</u> the <u>preposition phrase</u> in each sentence.

The man in the red jacket looks lost.

I was daydreaming about an enormous banquet.

Louis wandered slowly around the shimmering lake.

They filled three rubbish bags with empty plastic bottles.

The lamb they saw across the field looked really soft and fluffy.

Emilia saw something move beneath the murky, brown water.

A **noun phrase** is a group of words that includes a **noun** and **any words that describe it**. → an old, dusty book

Noun phrases can be expanded using **adjectives**, **preposition phrases** and **other nouns**.

the cat → the stripy, ginger cat with a bell on her collar

3 Underline the longest noun phrase in each sentence.

The cake with the chocolate icing is delicious.

The shark was swimming around a shoal of small, nervous fish.

We walked past a house with a big tree-house in the garden.

The brightly-coloured dragon swooped through the air.

Please can you pass me the purple hat from the top drawer?

4 Expand these noun phrases by adding an adjective and a preposition phrase to each one.

the donkey ➡ ....

a lizard ➡ ....

the peas ➡ ....

his glasses ➡ ....

the ceiling ➡ ....

 **Now Try This** Write a description of where you live, using expanded noun phrases to make your description as detailed as possible.

Section 2 — Phrases and Clauses

Clauses

A **main clause** has a **subject** and a **verb**, and **makes sense** on its own.

A **subordinate clause** gives extra information, but **doesn't make sense** on its own.

Tom played squash while Dan walked the dog.
main clause → ← subordinate clause

A **relative clause** is a type of **subordinate clause** that is often introduced by a **relative pronoun**.

I bought a car which had red wheels.
relative pronoun → ← relative clause

1) Write M for main clause or S for subordinate clause next to the clauses underlined below.

Mary ate lots of popcorn <u>while she watched the film</u>. ☐

<u>We like pizza</u>, but we love lasagne most of all. ☐

I think my teacher is secretly a spy, <u>although I'm not sure</u>. ☐

<u>I'm going out</u>, and I won't be back until after dinner. ☐

<u>If we leave now</u>, we'll be back in time for Lucy's party. ☐

2) Add a suitable relative clause to complete the sentences below.

I looked at Caroline, ... , and ran.

Liam read the sign, ... , very slowly.

We went to the shop, ... , with Shaun.

He met Sasha, ... , last year.

 **Now Try This** — Can you write a sentence that has a main clause, a subordinate clause, and a relative clause, as well as a noun phrase and a preposition phrase?

Section 2 — Phrases and Clauses

Section 3 — Linking Ideas

Conjunctions

Conjunctions are words or phrases that **join two sentences** or **two parts** of a sentence. They help your writing to **flow smoothly**, which is called **cohesion**.

He didn't want it. I ate it myself. It was delicious. ← This **doesn't** flow very well.

He didn't want it, so I ate it myself and it was delicious.
← This flows **much better**.

1) **Fill the gaps in this passage with the <u>conjunctions</u> below to improve its cohesion. Only use each conjunction <u>once</u>.**

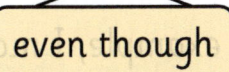 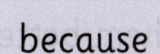  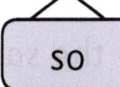 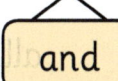

even though   because   as soon as   so   and

We're learning to grow fruits and vegetables .... we have a

new garden at school. Mr Beeman let us plant potatoes ....

we haven't done it before, ... Miss Everton says we can plant some

carrots .... we have time, ... we're getting the soil ready.

2) **Rewrite the passage below by adding some <u>conjunctions</u> to make it flow better.**

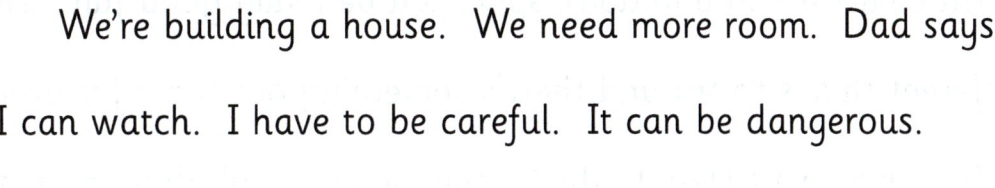

We're building a house. We need more room. Dad says I can watch. I have to be careful. It can be dangerous.

....

....

....

 **Write three simple sentences about your hobbies. Then, see how many different ways you can join them together using conjunctions.**

Linking Paragraphs with Adverbials

Adverbial phrases tell you *how, when, where* or *how often* something happens. They can be used to *link sentences* and *paragraphs* together.

I love sledging. In contrast, my best friend prefers skiing.

The *adverbial phrase* helps these *sentences* to *flow*. This is called cohesion.

1) Underline the adverbial phrases in this passage.

I do chores four times a week. Despite this, my sister gets more pocket money than me. Of course, if her chores were harder it would be fair. After all, I do the same jobs as her, and I do them better. For example, I make sure I wash up properly. My sister, on the other hand, makes a mess of it!

2) Circle the best word or phrase from the brackets to complete each paragraph.

There are many reasons why we need to have P.E. lessons in school.

(Firstly / However), it's important to keep healthy by doing regular exercise. It would be great for everyone to have the opportunity to keep fit.

(In contrast / In addition), sport can be really good fun. There are lots of different things to try and there's something out there for everyone.

(For example / Despite this), some people think that sport isn't as important as other subjects. They think P.E. lessons are a waste of time.

(After a while / However), I think that we need a balanced school day, both inside and outside the classroom.

 Write a passage about your school day, linking the sentences with adverbials.

Linking Paragraphs Using Repetition

Repeating a **word** or **phrase** is another way to **link sentences** and **paragraphs** together.

My sister Ava was born at 5:30 am. When Ava was born, I went to stay with my aunt and uncle for the night.

1) <u>Link</u> these paragraphs together using <u>one</u> of the repeated phrases on the right.

Living in London is fantastic because there's loads to do, including the theatre.

→ .... is also good because it's easy to travel by bus.

Loads to do
Living in London

Saturday is the best day of the week. I spend it at the football with Uncle Joe.

→ .... I buy a programme because I collect them.

At the football
The best day is

2) Write the <u>first sentence</u> of the <u>next paragraph</u> in each story. Include one <u>repeated</u> word or phrase.

Mrs Harrison knitted her grandson, Ben, a new bobble hat for winter. She thought it would match the lime green jumper she gave him last year.

....

....

Maisy had been staring out of the window of the car for what felt like ten years. They were still hours away from the hotel.

....

....

 **Continue one of the stories above, using repetition to link your paragraphs.**

Section 3 — Linking Ideas

Using Ellipsis

Ellipsis is when you remove unnecessary extra words or phrases from a sentence. It helps your sentences to flow smoothly.

Harry eats cake when he wants to eat cake. ← This doesn't flow very well.

Ellipsis also refers to the '...' punctuation.

Harry eats cake when he wants to. ← Removing 'eat cake' from the end of the sentence makes it flow better.

1) Cross out the unnecessary words in each sentence so that they flow smoothly.

She swam faster and she swam more gracefully than me.

I've been to Spain, but my parents haven't been to Spain.

She left the class because she wanted to leave the class.

2) Rewrite these sentences, removing the unnecessary words and phrases.

Polly loves baking cakes and she loves baking biscuits.

....

Gordon saw lots of monkeys, but Jade didn't see lots of monkeys.

....

I'm going to stay indoors, and I'm going to read a book.

....

Max showed Ian the kitchen, and he showed him the lounge.

....

 **Now Try This** Write a diary entry about the best day of your life. Use conjunctions, adverbials, repetition and ellipsis to make your writing flow smoothly.

Section 3 — Linking Ideas

Section 4 — Tenses

Present Tense and Past Tense

To write about something that happens regularly, use the simple present tense.

Nadeema visits her gran.   Mr Smith hears everything.

To write about something that's finished, use the simple past tense.

Nadeema visited her gran.   Mr Smith heard everything.

1) Tick the sentences that are in the simple present tense.

I get up at seven o'clock. ☐   They launched the rocket. ☐

Leon writes every day. ☐   We leave at half past one. ☐

The koala did a dance. ☐   Megan posted her letters. ☐

Rewrite the sentences you ticked so that they are in the simple past tense.

....

....

....

2) For each pair of words, write one simple present tense and one simple past tense sentence.

Jack golf →   Present: ....

Past: ....

we shop →   Present: ....

Past: ....

Now Try This — Write three sentences in the simple present tense, using a different verb in each one. Next, rewrite your sentences in the simple past tense.

Present and Past Progressive

To write about something that's still happening, use the present form of 'to be' plus the main verb with 'ing' on the end. This is called the present progressive.

are / am / is ➕ verb ➕ ing ⟶ Chloe is chatting.

The past progressive is formed like the present progressive, but 'to be' has to be in the past tense. ⟶ Leo was frying an egg.

1) Cross out the incorrect words to form the <u>past progressive</u>.

We (are / is / were) (plant / planting / plants) seeds.

I (am / was / were) (looking / look / looks) for my dad.

He (is / were / was) (ride / ridden / riding) a horse.

2) Form the present and past progressive by using the <u>correct form</u> of '<u>to be</u>' and the '<u>ing</u>' <u>form</u> of each verb.

verb	present progressive	past progressive
to go	Bob .... out.	Bob .... out.
to win	We .... the race.	We .... the race.
to drive	I .... to France.	I .... to France.
to shut	She .... a door.	She .... a door.
to knit	They .... hats.	They .... hats.

3) Write a <u>sentence</u> about what you <u>were doing</u> one hour ago.

....

 Use the past progressive to describe what you were doing at this time last week. Then, use the present progressive to describe what you are doing now.

Section 4 — Tenses

The Perfect Form

Use the **present perfect** form of a verb to talk about something that happened **before now**, but **not** at a **specific time**.

Riley has spilt his drink. ← We don't know exactly when he spilt the drink.

Use the **past perfect** form of a verb to talk about something that happened **before now**, and **before something else** happened.

Riley had spilt his drink when Mum arrived. ← We know that Riley spilt the drink **before his mother got there**.

1) Complete these sentences using the past perfect form of a suitable verb.

Corrie ....**had moved**.... to Belfast by the time she was six.

Steve was annoyed because Simon .... the film already.

Ruby .... me her old guitar before she bought a new one.

I .... my gran's letters in time for dinner.

2) Rewrite this passage using the present perfect form.

I visited my new school. I put my name down for the rugby team and Jon joined the art club. We spoke to our new teacher.

....

....

....

 Use the two events below to write two different sentences that use the past perfect form: 'Jerry hears a crash'   'the phone call ends'

Section 4 — Tenses

Section 5 — Sentence Structure

Subject and Object

A simple sentence has a **subject** and a **verb**. It usually has an **object**.

The **subject** is the person or thing doing the verb. It usually comes **first**.

The **object** usually comes **after** the verb. It has something **done to it** by the verb.

The **cat** drinks the **juice**.

The **verb** usually comes **after** the subject.

This is only true for active sentences. See page 24.

1) Circle the subject and underline the object in each of these sentences.

The fox crosses the road.

Hannah speaks to Samuel calmly.

The cat chases the squirrel.

Mairi forgot her sunglasses again.

Uncle Yuvi bought a sandwich.

The bear hugged the tree.

Yesterday Zoe read the newspaper.

The gardener carried the plant pots.

2) Label the underlined parts of each sentence as either subject, object or verb.

The swimmer splashed the children.

The baker dropped the egg.

The grocer shouted at Niamh.

Shweta sings pop songs.

Stephanie met Mr Potter.

Kathryn bought a dress.

23

3) **Complete** each sentence by **writing** in a **subject** or an **object**.

- subject → .... wrote a newspaper article.
- object → Sian threw .... across the field.
- object → The teacher laughed at ....
- subject → .... made a cheesecake.
- object → Mrs Huckton broke ....
- subject → .... climbed the tree.

4) **Choose** the correct word or phrase from the balloons to **complete** each sentence. Then **label** the word you've added as **subject**, **verb** or **object**.

Rob .... to the airport.

A group of girls .... the ice cream.

.... built a nest in the apple tree.

Francesca opened .... nervously.

.... doesn't like Sam any more.

Balloons: Mia, the door, a bird, ate, drove

Now Try This — Write two sentences containing the word 'crocodile'. In one sentence, it should be the subject, and in the other it should be the object.

Section 5 — Sentence Structure

Passive and Active Voice

In **active** sentences, the **subject** of the sentence **does something** to the object.

Rivka plays **the violin.**
subject — object

In **passive** sentences, something **is done to** the subject.

The violin was played **by Rivka.**
subject — The word '**by**' can introduce **who** does the **action**.

1 In the boxes write '**A**' for the active sentences and '**P**' for the passive ones.

The Queen wears a crown. ☐   Nick was pushed by Cameron. ☐
The cleaner scrubbed the floor. ☐   The chicken crossed the road. ☐
The room was tidied by Tim. ☐   The leaf was blown in the wind. ☐
The balloon was filled with air. ☐   Amy wore a red dress. ☐
Martha tried to catch it. ☐   The speech was made by Tony. ☐
Ashok bought a new hat. ☐   My dad was awarded a medal. ☐

2 Unscramble the words in each box to write a passive sentence.

David   letter   by   the   signed   was

....

men   the   delivered   was   the   by   sofa

....

Antonio   with   was   a   hit   pillow

....

Section 5 — Sentence Structure

3 Rewrite each sentence, changing it from active to passive.

Imani heard the bell.

The bell was heard by Imani.

Auntie Pam hugged Eleanor.

....

Paul found Fiona in the garden.

....

Lizzie picked up Prisha and Olivia.

....

The postman shouted at the dog.

....

4 Underline all of the passive sentences in this passage.

The first match was won by Lonsdale Lions. However, Tappleby Tigers then signed the Lions' star player. The Lions were defeated by the Tigers in the second game. The Tigers won the trophy and celebrated with a big party. During the party, the trophy was stolen by a magpie. Thankfully, the police caught the magpie. The trophy was returned to the Tigers by PC Harley.

Now rewrite the passive sentences as active sentences.

....

....

....

....

Section 5 — Sentence Structure

5

Write 'A' next to the active sentences and 'P' next to the passive ones. Then, label the underlined parts of each sentence as either subject or object.

Advit plays <u>the piano</u>. [A]
→ ....object....

<u>Toby</u> was given the letter. [ ]
→ ....

<u>The ball</u> was thrown. [ ]
→ ....

<u>The dog</u> sniffed the acorns. [ ]
→ ....

Pete fixed <u>the window</u>. [ ]
→ ....

<u>The cake</u> was eaten by Jo. [ ]
→ ....

6

Rewrite the active sentences below as passive sentences. Don't include the person doing the action.

The chef stirred the sauce.

The sauce was stirred.

The mayor welcomed the visitors.

....

Marilyn chased the dog down the road.

....

Mr Grey banned fizzy drinks at school.

....

Now Try This — Newspaper headlines often use the passive voice. Write the opening to a news article, using a passive headline and an active introductory sentence.

Section 5 — Sentence Structure

Section 6 — Writing Style

Formal and Informal Writing

Formal vocabulary is used when you're writing something important. It can sound quite serious.

Kaia is making me extremely angry.

Formal writing doesn't use apostrophes for shortened versions of words, so you need to say 'He is', not 'He's'.

Informal vocabulary is chattier and friendlier.

Kaia's driving me round the bend.

Informal writing can include shortened versions of words and informal phrases.

1 For each pair of sentences, write 'F' next to the formal version and 'I' next to the informal version.

You can't come with us. ☐
You cannot accompany us. ☐

We really must hurry. ☐
Come on, we'll be late. ☐

That is unacceptable, Mother. ☐
That's not OK, Mum. ☐

Pop along to reception first. ☐
Please report to reception. ☐

Stephen's got some new wheels. ☐
Stephen has bought a new car. ☐

I need to find some money. ☐
I need to grab some cash. ☐

2 Underline the words that make each of these sentences informal.

Harjot was chuffed when he won.

The girls nattered constantly.

He is bringing the stuff over later.

Grab that box over there.

There are plenty of cakes, ta.

This is way better than last time.

Our new defender is a corker.

I am shattered after that journey.

Blimey, be careful with that!

Stop gadding about and sit still.

Formal writing doesn't usually use exclamation marks. **Question marks** can be used as long as the questions are **polite**. → Would you like some tea?

Informal writing can include **contractions**. → We'll see you there.

Some **very formal** writing uses the **subjunctive form**. This uses subject-verb pairs like '**I were**' and '**had I**'. → Had I known, I would not have gone.

Questions are often added to the end of **statements** in **informal writing**. → You'd like some tea, wouldn't you?

3) Draw lines to join each informal sentence with the matching formal one.

He's coming over later.   Do you think that is fair?
Did they have any cash?   He is coming over later.
That's not fair, is it?   Had they any money?

4) Write 'F' next to the formal sentences and 'I' next to the informal sentences. Then rewrite the informal sentences to make them formal.

Do you wish to dance? ☐

....

She should've taken an umbrella. ☐

....

We're meeting them at the park, aren't we? ☐

....

Mrs Hudson received a present from her friend. ☐

....

If I were to move abroad, I would live in Spain. ☐

....

5 Complete the crossword by finding a formal word that means the same as the underlined informal word or phrase in each clue.

Across
1. Grace was <u>gutted</u> after the match.
2. Hazel and Andrew are going to <u>tie the knot</u>.
3. The <u>kids</u> were very noisy.
4. You should <u>chill out</u>.

Down
1. Dhruv <u>nicked</u> a biscuit from the plate.
2. Your <u>mum</u> is going to be upset.
3. I was <u>shattered</u> after the sleepover.
4. Timmy's hands are very <u>grubby</u>.

6 For each sentence, <u>choose</u> a word from the brackets to <u>fill</u> the gap so that the sentence is <u>formal</u>.

Kimberley's work was .... (lousy / unacceptable)

The firework display will be .... (wicked / wonderful)

I .... that Liverton will win the league this year. (think / reckon)

Chris is .... to go to America. (hoping / bursting)

This Geography homework is .... (easy-peasy / simple)

I wish you would stop .... (complaining / whingeing)

 Find a magazine article and see if you can underline ten informal words.

Section 6 — Writing Style

Writing for Your Audience

The audience of a piece of writing is the person or people who read it. You need to make sure that your writing is suitable for that audience.

Formal writing is used for reports, essays and letters to people you don't know.

Informal writing is used for writing where you know your audience, for example a letter to a friend.

You should use formal language in most of your writing.

1) Decide if each text would use formal or informal writing and draw a line to the correct ring.

A letter of complaint to a company.

A postcard to your sister.

A report on rainforests.

An essay about ancient Egypt.

A note for your friend.

A text message to your mum.

2) Write 'F' next to the formal texts and 'I' next to the informal texts.

A note to the milkman asking for an extra pint of milk.

A letter to the Queen asking her to visit your school.

A letter to your teacher to apologise for being late.

An email to your auntie asking how her cat is.

A school report about the life cycle of a frog.

An email inviting your friends over for dinner.

3) Tick the sentence that you would be most likely to find in each text type.

A text message to your friend
Thanks for coming mate — it was fab. ☐
Thank you for a delightful evening, my dear friend. ☐

A school science report
That's the coolest experiment we've ever done. ☐
We found the experiment very interesting. ☐

A letter to a politician
Don't forget to reply to my letter. ☐
I look forward to receiving your reply. ☐

An email to your brother
Have you acquired my football boots? ☐
You've nicked my footy boots, haven't you? ☐

4) Rewrite each sentence so that it is more appropriate for the type of writing given.

An email to a friend
I cannot believe that you did not come.
....

A letter of complaint
I've never had such a disgusting meal.
....

A letter to the Prime Minister
You're going to ban homework, right?
....

A note to your mum
I request that you pick me up from school at 4 pm.
....

A report about the Victorians
Loads of kids cleaned chimneys and stuff.
....

Now Try This — Now try writing a formal letter to your favourite author.

Standard and Non-Standard English

Standard English is the type of English you should use in your **written** work. It helps make your writing **clearer**.

Standard English → Did you see anything? I have not found him.

non-Standard English → I didn't see nothing. We ain't found him.

1 Draw lines to show which word completes these sentences in Standard English.

I've asked Zayan to speak to ………… farmers.

Penny hasn't heard back from ………… yet.

How did ………… potatoes get there?

Kathy will pick ………… up from the station.

I hate peas, but my sister Roz loves ………… .

them   **those**

2 Write '2' next to the double negative sentences and '1' next to those with one negative.

Nobody can do nothing to stop the floods. ☐

I haven't got no time to do my homework. ☐

Joseph couldn't find anywhere to stay. ☐

Maria doesn't want nobody to leave yet. ☐

Don't do nothing until we get to the party. ☐

You can't tell anyone what I said. ☐

Mum said I mustn't climb trees no more. ☐

A double negative is non-Standard English.

Section 6 — Writing Style

3) Draw lines to match each sentence with its Standard English form.

You should of gone too.   —   I might have put it away.

He could of helped.   —   She will have gone by now.

I might of put it away.   —   He could have helped.

She will of gone by now.   —   You should have gone too.

4) Cross out the incorrect options so that each sentence is in Standard English.

Grandma (saw / seen) the picture that Josh had (did / done).

The sisters (saw / seen) a ballet which (come / came) to their local theatre.

Hattie (done / did) lots of work, but then she (gone / went) home.

Hassan and Chima have (seen / saw) the person who (did / done) it.

Eshe and Phil have (come / came) to visit, but they have (gone / went) out.

5) Rewrite each of these sentences so that they are in Standard English.

He ain't coming on holiday with us.

....

I ain't impressed with this weather.

....

Stefan ain't seen the film yet.

....

I ain't found the lost rabbit.

....

Section 6 — Writing Style

6

Tick the box under '**I**' or '**me**' to complete each sentence in **Standard English**.

	I	me
Charlotte and .... went for a walk.	☐	☐
Kofi shouted at Annabel and	☐	☐
Alice and .... were late for dinner.	☐	☐
.... ran to collect the parcels.	☐	☐
The teacher said it was up to	☐	☐

'I' is always the subject. 'Me' is always the object.

7

In each sentence, **underline** the **verb** that **doesn't agree** with the **subject**. **Write out** the verb as it **should** appear on the dotted line.

Jonathan and Maya goes weightlifting on Thursdays. ➡ ....

Ellie play cello in the orchestra. ➡ ....

Neil and Nadia is performing on the stage. ➡ ....

They was planning a party for Saturday night. ➡ ....

Fernando have a new haircut. ➡ ....

Kalifa and Freya has gone to Africa. ➡ ....

8

Draw lines to match each sentence with its **Standard English** form.

Them robbers stole my bag!	Aren't you helping?
I don't wanna go.	We're not bothering anyone.
Ain't you helping?	I don't want to go.
We're not bothering no one.	Those robbers stole my bag!

Section 6 — Writing Style

9 Choose a word from the fish to complete each sentence in **Standard English**.

Fish words: those, saw, was, of, me, were, have, I, seen, them

Dad said we should .... asked for directions to the campsite.

They .... at our house for ages and ate ten bowls of custard each.

My friend Yared and .... are practising for a three-legged race.

Yesterday I .... a fantastic circus performer breathe fire!

Do you like .... trousers or do you want to keep looking?

My cousin Aanya gave .... two pounds for my piggy bank.

The film is so good that we have .... it three times already.

10 Write out each sentence below in **Standard English**.

I think my leg is broke. ....

Have you found them geese? ....

It weren't my fault! ....

We been walking for hours. ....

The puppy licked Jake and I. ....

I ain't done nothing. ....

They could of asked us. ....

Now Try This — "You and me need to find that gnome." Why is it non-Standard English to use 'me' in this sentence? Can you rewrite the sentence in Standard English?

Section 6 — Writing Style

Glossary

Adjective — A word that describes a noun, e.g. **slow** snail, **big** tree.

Adverb — A word that describes a **verb**, an **adjective** or other **adverbs**.

Adverbial — A group of words that behaves like an **adverb**.

Antonyms — Words that mean the opposite, e.g. **loud** and **quiet**.

Clause — Part of a sentence that contains a **subject** and a **verb**.

Conjunction — A word or phrase that **joins** two parts of a sentence.

Ellipses — Removing a word that you would **expect** to be included.

Fronted adverbial — An adverbial that comes at the **start** of a sentence.

Main clause — A clause that **makes sense** on its own, e.g. We play outside when it is not raining.

Noun — A word that **names** something, e.g. **Dan**, **hat**, **Newcastle**.

Object — The part of the sentence having **something done to it**.

Preposition — Introduces a **pronoun**, **noun** or **noun phrase** and tells you **where**, **when** or **why** something happens, e.g. I am in front of the gate.

Pronoun — A word used to **replace** a **noun**, e.g. **it**, **we**, **you**.

Subject — The person or thing **doing the verb**.

Subordinate clause — A clause that **doesn't make sense** on its own, e.g. We play outside when it is not raining.

Synonyms — Words that mean the same, e.g. **large** and **big**.

Verb — A doing or being word, e.g. **sit**, **practise**, **remember**, **is**.

Answers

Section 1 – Word Types

Page 4 – Nouns

1. You should have underlined: **zoo, lions, monkeys, Ella, animals**.
   You should have circled: **excitement, childhood, courage**.
2. Any suitable nouns. Examples:
   Everyone feels so much **happiness** about doing more drawings of **cats**.
   The **team** of **cyclists** moves really slowly along the **road**.
   A group of **humans** could be called a **crowd**.

Page 5 – Adjectives

1. You should have underlined: **cold, dark, howling, leafless, torrential, little, jittery, creaking, tired, old**.
2. Any suitable adjectives. Examples:
   The **golden** sun shone brightly over the **green** valley and the **hungry** cows stood munching the **long** grass.
3. Any suitable sentence. Example:
   The silly, bossy boy made a nasty comment.

Page 6 – Verbs

1. Laurie often **goes** to the shop and **buys** some bread.
   We always **visit** Habeeb at the weekend and **take** him out.
   The cows **eat** the grass and **watch** the walkers go by.
2. Any suitable sentences. Examples:
   Ruth's pony smiled and she saw all his teeth.
   The mole claps whenever he sees the sun.
   Dylan cries when his TV breaks.
3. You should have underlined: **I shall have pizza for dinner tomorrow.**

Page 7 – Adverbs

1. Any suitable adverbs. Examples:
   Jarome **suddenly** decided to book a holiday to Wales.
   The girls **secretively** passed a note to the boys.
   Mum and Dad are **really** pleased with me.
   The test was **extremely** difficult.
   I will **definitely** tell Katie the truth tomorrow.
   The teacher jumped **excitedly** onto the bus.
2. Any suitable sentence. Example:
   Jill was really surprised — Edward was probably going to win the race now.

Pages 8 and 9 – Synonyms and Antonyms

1. **front — back, big — small, hot — cold, dry — wet**
2. Marvin feels drowsy — he's just so **sleepy** today.
   They live in a huge house — it's simply **enormous**.
   The party was quite rowdy — people kept saying how **noisy** it was.
3. She always exaggerates her achievements — she's so **arrogant**.
   I think Humphrey is a bit strange — his behaviour is very **curious**.
   There are few birds around here. In fact, their numbers are **sparse**.
4. Across: 1 **first**, 2 **happy**, 3 **early**, 4 **high**, 5 **wrong**
   Down: 1 **fast**, 2 **hard**, 3 **take**, 4 **tiny**, 5 **rich**
5. Adjective: **simple**
   Any suitable synonyms and antonyms. Examples:
   Synonym: **easy**
   Antonym: **hard**
   Adverb: **quickly**
   Any suitable synonyms and antonyms. Examples:
   Synonym: **speedily**
   Antonym: **slowly**
6. Any suitable sentences. Examples:
   We are so **near** to the end now.
   Louise is a **lovely** girl.

Page 10 – Determiners

1. Any suitable determiners. Examples:
   Which key opens **this** door?
   The seagull stole **four** chips from **that** person over there.
   I read **her** book and would like to ask **some** questions.
2. That dog wants to eat this sandwich I brought for my lunch.
   Which shoes should I wear for your birthday party this afternoon?
   Today, some chickens escaped from their coop and ran into the village.
3. Any sensible determiners and nouns. Examples:
   To make the biscuits, you will need **two eggs**.
   I must remember to take **my notebook** with me tomorrow.
   Jonah couldn't believe he'd finally seen **the castle**.

Page 11 – Pronouns

1. My dog Rover hates going for walks along the path **which** runs by the canal. When **we** walk there, he barks a lot, especially when he sees Mr Mildew, **whose** Poodle then starts woofing back at us. After a while, Mrs Waterweed, **who** lives in a canal boat, always opens her window and shouts at **us**.
2. Carrie decided to do it herself.
   Some stories are fictional, others are based on real events.
   The dog scratched itself when nobody was looking.
   The children tasted all of the cakes but thought theirs were the best.

Section 2 – Phrases and Clauses

Pages 12 and 13 – Phrases

1. You should have ticked: **under the bed, in the garden, big birds of prey, through the woods, on the top shelf**.
2. In the sentences below, the preposition is in **bold** and the preposition phrase is underlined:
   The man **in** the red jacket looks lost.
   I was daydreaming **about** an enormous banquet.
   Louis wandered slowly **around** the shimmering lake.
   They filled three rubbish bags **with** empty plastic bottles.
   The lamb they saw **across** the field looked really soft and fluffy.
   Emilia saw something move **beneath** the murky, brown water.

3. You should have underlined these phrases:
   The cake with the chocolate icing is delicious.
   The shark was swimming around a shoal of small, nervous fish.
   We walked past a house with a big tree-house in the garden.
   The brightly-coloured dragon swooped through the air.
   Please can you pass me the purple hat from the top drawer?

4. Any suitable expanded noun phrases that include an adjective and a preposition phrase. Examples:
   the cheeky donkey next to the gate
   the intricately-decorated ceiling with a disco ball
   a green lizard in the desert sand
   the mushy peas sliding around her plate
   his blue glasses on the table

Page 14 – Clauses

1. Main clauses: **We like pizza, I'm going out**
   Subordinate clauses: **while she watched the film, although I'm not sure, If we leave now**

2. Any suitable relative clauses. Examples:
   I looked at Caroline, **who seemed very angry**, and ran.
   Liam read the sign, **which was in French**, very slowly.
   We went to the shop, **which sells comics**, with Shaun.
   He met Sasha, **who moved here from Russia**, last year.

Section 3 – Linking Ideas

Page 15 – Conjunctions

1. We're learning to grow fruits and vegetables **because** we have a new garden at school. Mr Beeman let us plant potatoes **even though** we haven't done it before, **and** Miss Everton says we can plant some carrots **as soon as** we have time, **so** we're getting the soil ready.

2. Example:
   We're building a house because we need more room.
   Dad says I can watch, but I have to be careful since it can be dangerous.

Page 16 – Linking Paragraphs with Adverbials

1. You should have underlined these phrases:
   I do chores four times a week. Despite this, my sister gets more pocket money than me. Of course, if her chores were harder it would be fair. After all, I do the same jobs as her, and I do them better. For example, I make sure I wash up properly. My sister, on the other hand, makes a mess of it!

2.   There are many reasons why we need to have P.E. lessons in school.
   Firstly, it's important to keep healthy by doing regular exercise. It would be great for everyone to have the opportunity to keep fit.
   In addition, sport can be really good fun. There are lots of different things to try and there's something out there for everyone.
   Despite this, some people think that sport isn't as important as other subjects. They think P.E. lessons are a waste of time.
   However, I think that we need a balanced school day, both inside and outside the classroom.

Page 17 – Linking Paragraphs Using Repetition

1. You should have written these phrases:
   Living in London
   At the football

2. Any sentences which link to the previous paragraph and use a repeated word or phrase. Examples:
   Her grandson, Ben, didn't wear the jumper, even though she thought he wore it every day.
   The hotel was in Sunderland, on top of a high hill.

Page 18 – Using Ellipsis

1. You should have crossed out these phrases:
   She swam faster and ~~she swam~~ more gracefully than me.
   I've been to Spain, but my parents haven't ~~been to Spain~~.
   She left the class because she wanted to ~~leave the class~~.

2. Polly loves baking cakes and biscuits.
   Gordon saw lots of monkeys, but Jade didn't.
   I'm going to stay indoors and read a book.
   (OR) I'm going to stay indoors to read a book.
   Max showed Ian the kitchen and the lounge.

Section 4 – Tenses

Page 19 – Present Tense and Past Tense

1. You should have ticked these sentences:
   I get up at seven o'clock.
   Leon writes every day.
   We leave at half past one.
   Rewritten sentences:
   I got up at seven o'clock.
   Leon wrote every day.
   We left at half past one.

2. Any sentences which use the words in the boxes and are in the correct tense. Examples:
   Present: Jack plays golf.
   Past: Jack played golf.
   Present: We go to the shop.
   Past: We went to the shop.

Page 20 – Present and Past Progressive

1. You should have crossed out these words:
   We (~~are~~ / ~~is~~ / were) (~~plant~~ / planting / ~~plants~~) seeds.
   I (am / was / ~~were~~) (looking / ~~look~~ / ~~looks~~) for my dad.
   He (~~is~~ / ~~were~~ / was) (~~ride~~ / ~~ridden~~ / riding) a horse.

2.
verb	present progressive	past progressive
to go	Bob is going out.	Bob was going out.
to win	We are winning the race.	We were winning the race.
to drive	I am driving to France.	I was driving to France.
to shut	She is shutting a door.	She was shutting a door.
to knit	They are knitting hats.	They were knitting hats.

3. Any sentence which uses at least one 'ing' verb in the past tense. Example:
I was reading a book.

Page 21 – The Perfect Form

1. Each sentence should have been completed with a past perfect form of a sensible verb, e.g.
Steve was annoyed because Simon <u>had seen</u> the film already.
Ruby <u>had given</u> me her old guitar before she bought a new one.
I <u>had delivered</u> my gran's letters in time for dinner.

2. I have visited my new school. I have put my name down for the rugby team and Jon has joined the art club. We have spoken to our new teacher.

Section 5 – Sentence Structure

Pages 22 and 23 – Subject and Object

1. In the sentences below, the subject is in **bold** and the object is underlined.
The fox crosses <u>the road</u>.
Hannah speaks to <u>Samuel</u> calmly.
The cat chases <u>the squirrel</u>.
Mairi forgot <u>her sunglasses</u> again.
Uncle Yuvi bought <u>a sandwich</u>.
The bear hugged <u>the tree</u>.
Yesterday **Zoe** read <u>the newspaper</u>.
The gardener carried <u>the plant pots</u>.

2. You should have labelled the words like this:
The swimmer — subject   the children — object
The baker — subject   the egg — object
The grocer — subject   shouted — verb
sings — verb   pop songs — object
met — verb   Mr Potter — object
Kathryn — subject   a dress — object

3. Each sentence should have been completed with a sensible suggestion, e.g.
Stephen wrote a newspaper article.
Sian threw **a ball** across the field.
The teacher laughed at **the joke**.
Grandma made a cheesecake.
Mrs Huckton broke **her arm**.
The monkey climbed the tree.

4. Rob <u>drove</u> to the airport. (verb)
A group of girls <u>ate</u> the ice cream. (verb)
<u>A bird</u> built a nest in the apple tree. (subject)
Francesca opened <u>the door</u> nervously. (object)
<u>Mia</u> doesn't like Sam any more. (subject)

Pages 24 to 26 – Passive and Active Voice

1. The Queen wears a crown. A
The cleaner scrubbed the floor. A
The room was tidied by Tim. P
The balloon was filled with air. P
Martha tried to catch it. A
Ashok bought a new hat. A
Nick was pushed by Cameron. P
The chicken crossed the road. A
The leaf was blown in the wind. P
Amy wore a red dress. A
The speech was made by Tony. P
My dad was awarded a medal. P

2. The letter was signed by David.
The sofa was delivered by the men.
Antonio was hit with a pillow.

3. The sentences should have been rewritten as follows:
Eleanor was hugged by Auntie Pam.
Fiona was found in the garden by Paul.
Prisha and Olivia were picked up by Lizzie.
The dog was shouted at by the postman.

4. You should have underlined these sentences:
The first match was won by Lonsdale Lions.
The Lions were defeated by the Tigers in the second game.
During the party, the trophy was stolen by a magpie.
The trophy was returned to the Tigers by PC Harley.
The sentences should have been rewritten as follows:
Lonsdale Lions won the first match.
The Tigers defeated the Lions in the second game.
During the party, a magpie stole the trophy.
PC Harley returned the trophy to the Tigers.

5. You should have labelled the words like this:
<u>Toby</u> was given the letter. — P, subject
<u>The ball</u> was thrown. — P, subject
<u>The dog</u> sniffed the acorns. — A, subject
Pete fixed <u>the window</u>. — A, object
<u>The cake</u> was eaten by Jo. — P, subject

6. The visitors were welcomed.
The dog was chased down the road.
Fizzy drinks were banned at school.

Section 6 – Writing Style

Pages 27 to 29 – Formal and Informal Writing

1. You can't come with us. — I
You cannot accompany us. — F
That is unacceptable, Mother. — F
That's not OK, Mum. — I
Stephen's got some new wheels. — I
Stephen has bought a new car. — F
We really must hurry. — F
Come on, we'll be late. — I
Pop along to reception first. — I
Please report to reception. — F
I need to find some money. — F
I need to grab some cash. — I

2. You should have underlined these words:
chuffed, stuff, ta, corker, Blimey, nattered, Grab, way, shattered, gadding

3. You should have matched these pairs:
He's coming over later. — He is coming over later.
Did they have any cash? — Had they any money?
That's not fair, is it? — Do you think that is fair?

4. Do you wish to dance? — F
She should've taken an umbrella. — I
We're meeting them at the park, aren't we? — I
Mrs Hudson received a present from her friend. — F
If I were to move abroad, I would live in Spain. — F
Examples of corrected sentences:
She should have taken an umbrella.
Are we meeting them at the park?

5. Across: 1: disappointed   3: children
            2: marry   4: relax
   Down: 1: stole   3: tired
            2: mother   4: dirty
6. unacceptable, wonderful, think, hoping, simple, complaining

Pages 30 and 31 – Writing for Your Audience

1. A letter of complaint to a company. — formal writing
   A postcard to your sister. — informal writing
   A report on rainforests. — formal writing
   An essay about ancient Egypt. — formal writing
   A note for your friend. — informal writing
   A text message to your mum. — informal writing

2. A note to the milkman asking for an extra pint of milk. — I
   A letter to the Queen asking her to visit your school. — F
   A letter to your teacher to apologise for being late. — F
   An email to your auntie asking how her cat is. — I
   A school report about the life cycle of a frog. — F
   An email inviting your friends over for dinner. — I

3. You should have ticked these sentences:
   Thanks for coming mate — it was fab.
   We found the experiment very interesting.
   I look forward to receiving your reply.
   You've nicked my footy boots, haven't you?

4. Example sentences:
   I can't believe you didn't make it.
   I have never eaten food of such a low standard.
   Are you going to ban homework?
   Can you pick me up from school at 4?
   Many children had to clean chimneys.

Pages 32 to 35 – Standard and Non-Standard English

1. I've asked Zayan to speak to ___ farmers. — those
   Penny hasn't heard back from ___ yet. — them
   How did ___ potatoes get there? — those
   Kathy will pick ___ up from the station. — them
   I hate peas, but my sister Roz loves ___ . — them

2. Nobody can do nothing to stop the floods. — 2
   I haven't got no time to do my homework. — 2
   Joseph couldn't find anywhere to stay. — 1
   Maria doesn't want nobody to leave yet. — 2
   Don't do nothing until we get to the party. — 2
   You can't tell anyone what I said. — 1
   Mum said I mustn't climb trees no more. — 2

3. You should have matched these pairs:
   You should of gone too. — You should have gone too.
   He could of helped. — He could have helped.
   I might of put it away. — I might have put it away.
   She will of gone by now. — She will have gone by now.

4. Grandma (saw / ~~seen~~) the picture that Josh had (~~did~~ / done).
   The sisters (saw / ~~seen~~) a ballet which (~~come~~ / came) to their local theatre.
   Hattie (~~done~~ / did) lots of work, but then she (~~gone~~ / went) home.
   Hassan and Chima have (seen / ~~saw~~) the person who (did / ~~done~~) it.
   Eshe and Phil have (come / ~~came~~) to visit, but they have (gone / ~~went~~) out.

5. Example sentences:
   He isn't coming on holiday with us.
   I am not impressed with this weather.
   Stefan hasn't seen the film yet.
   I haven't found the lost rabbit.

6. Charlotte and ___ went for a walk. — I
   Kofi shouted at Annabel and ___ . — me
   Alice and ___ were late for dinner. — I
   ___ ran to collect the parcels. — I
   The teacher said it was up to ___ . — me

7. goes — go
   play — plays
   is — are
   was — were
   have — has
   has — have

8. You should have matched these pairs:
   Them robbers stole my bag! — Those robbers stole my bag!
   I don't wanna go. — I don't want to go.
   Ain't you helping? — Aren't you helping?
   We're not bothering no one. — We're not bothering anyone.

9. Dad said we should **have** asked for directions to the campsite.
   They **were** at our house for ages and ate ten bowls of custard each.
   My friend Yared and **I** are practising for a three-legged race.
   Yesterday I **saw** a fantastic circus performer breathe fire!
   Do you like **those** trousers or do you want to keep looking?
   My cousin Aanya gave **me** two pounds for my piggy bank.
   The film is so good that we have **seen** it three times already.

10. I think my leg is broken.
    Have you found those geese?
    It wasn't my fault!
    We have been walking for hours. / We were walking for hours.
    The puppy licked Jake and me.
    I haven't done anything.
    They could have asked us.

Answers